By a masterly irony, the motto of Maria Fitzherbert's family was *Regi semper fidelis* – always faithful to the King. None would be more faithful to her King nor suffer more for that fidelity than Maria herself, whom George ever regarded as the true 'wife of my heart and soul'. But not only had the heir to the throne married without the Sovereign's permission, Maria was also a Roman Catholic. Their marriage was an open secret, but the British constitution would not recognize its validity, and the most powerful families in the land were united in their efforts to expunge it from history.

THE WIDOW AND THE RAKE

MARIA SMYTHE MADE HER MARK ON LONDON AS RESPECTABLE MRS FITZHERBERT, THE POPULAR SOCIETY HOSTESS, WHILE GEORGE, THE PRINCE OF WALES, WAS ALREADY RENOWNED FOR HIS EXTRAVAGANCE AND LOOSE LIVING

MARIA WAS BORN INTO A PROMINENT ROMAN Catholic family in July 1756, the eldest of Walter Smythe and Mary Errington's six children. At that time, Walter and Mary were living in the north of England, but they later settled permanently at Brambridge, near Winchester in Hampshire, in a roomy mansion set in spacious grounds. Here were born Maria's four brothers and her sister.

When she was old enough – possibly nine or ten – Maria was sent to an Ursuline convent school in the Faubourg Sainte-Antoine in Paris. On one of her holidays, her parents took Maria to Versailles to watch Louis XV dine in public. Watching the King at the dinner table was a sort of spectator sport in those days. People bought tickets and stood quietly behind a barrier, under strict instructions not to disturb the Royal repast. Unfortunately, little Maria did just that. As Louis

Maria is popularly supposed to have been born in the Red Room at Tong Castle below, having arrived unexpectedly while her parents were visiting the Duke of Kingston. Right Maria's father Walter Smythe wearing the uniform of an officer in the Austrian army. Like many British Catholics – then a persecuted sect barred from the army, the navy, the law or parliament – he sought employment abroad. Far right Mrs Weld. This portrait of Maria was painted by Sir Joshua Reynolds at the time of her short-lived first marriage. The Weld family tradition records that Maria was furious with the artist, indignantly saying that Reynolds had given her a grey wig

tore a piece of chicken apart with his fingers, Maria burst into peals of laughter. Her parents were mortified by this breach of etiquette, but Louis found it amusing. To show there was no offence taken, he sent out a nobleman, the Duke of Soubise, with a dish of sugar plums for her. Many years later, when the Duke was an old man and Maria Fitzherbert was a guest at the French court, they reminisced about this incident.

At the age of 16, Maria returned to Brambridge, where her cascading golden hair, flawless complexion and full figure, allied with an unaffected *joie de vivre*, soon made her eminently eligible among the unattached young Catholic gentlemen of the day.

In the event, it was an older man who first won her hand in marriage. Edward Weld of Lulworth Castle, Dorset, a rich childless widower,

Mansell

Sotheby's

👑 *Queen Charlotte commissioned this beeswax model of the baby Prince George lying on a velvet couch* left *as a present to her husband, George III. The model is about four inches long and the Queen seems to have kept it for herself, as she had it constantly on her dressing-table at Buckingham House, under a glass bell-jar*

'*Rather above the common size, his limbs well proportioned, and upon the whole well made, though rather too great a penchant to grow fat...*'

THE PRINCE OF WALES ON HIMSELF

infection and he and Maria decided to spend the winter in the more temperate climes of the south of France. In Nice, on 7 May, Maria became a widow for the second time when Thomas died at the age of 37. His will left her well provided for, with nearly £2000 a year and the house in Park Street, but this was scant compensation for the loss of a genuinely beloved husband. Unwilling to return to England, Maria remained abroad for almost a year, working in Nice and in Paris for a charity for English Catholic orphans.

In 1782 she finally returned to England, living first in Brighton, then at Marble Hill in Richmond. Friends tried to tempt her back into London society, but she thought it disrespectful to the memory of her late husband to be seen enjoying herself in public.

Back in society
Two years passed before she moved back to Park Street and the following notice appeared in the *Morning Herald* of 20 March 1784: 'Mrs Fitzherbert is arrived in London for the season.' Her 'coming out' was an immediate success. On 27 July the *Herald* reported that 'The Widow of

was 44 and Maria was 18 when they married early in 1775. Like most marriages of the time, it was an arranged match, but the new Mrs Weld was extremely contented amid the opulent surroundings of Lulworth. A neighbour recalls her at dinner on her 19th birthday, 'perfectly unaffected and unassuming in manner'. But the idyll was not to last. Before the year was out Edward Weld had died after a riding accident, without making provision in his will for his new bride. Lulworth Castle passed to Edward's brother, and Maria returned to Brambridge.

Her youth and looks ensured a plentiful supply of suitors, and three years later she married Thomas Fitzherbert of Swynnerton in Staffordshire. She was 21 and he was 32. Fitzherbert was more worldly and better connected than Edward Weld. He and Maria entertained lavishly at Swynnerton and enjoyed the company of Protestants as well as Catholics in their London house in Park Street, Mayfair. This period coincided with the repeal or relaxation of many anti-Catholic laws and Maria's religion ceased to be a stigma, at least in the enlightened salons of high-society London.

But time was running out for Maria's marriage. In early 1781, Thomas fell ill with a lung

Mansell

By gracious permission of HM the Queen

♛ *The family of George III, painted in 1770 by John Zoffany above. The portrait shows King George and Queen Charlotte with their six eldest children, dressed in the richly colourful 17th-century costumes made popular by Van Dyck's portraits. Prince Frederick – later the Duke of York , immortalized in a satirical popular rhyme for his uneventful military career – stands between his father and the eight-year-old Prince of Wales, who is dressed in scarlet. Prince William, later William IV, is seated on the left, playing with a cockatoo. Queen Victoria's father Edward, aged three, sits on the floor with a King Charles spaniel puppy, while Princess Charlotte and baby Augusta are posed gracefully at their mother's knee*

♛ *King George and Queen Charlotte bought Buckingham House left in 1762 as a family home. George IV planned to turn it into a palace, but died before Nash's designs were completed*

the late Mr. F-h-t has in her train half of our young Nobility.' At around this time, she agreed to accompany her uncle, Henry Errington, to the Royal Opera House. Among the audience that night was the 21-year-old Prince of Wales, whose eye for a pretty lady was already legendary.

George Augustus Frederick, Prince of Wales, Earl of Chester, Duke of Cornwall, Duke of Rothesay, Earl of Carrick and Baron of Renfrew, was considered a rake of the first order by the time he saw Maria Fitzherbert. He was born on 12 August 1762 at St James's Palace, the eldest of George III and Queen Charlotte's 15 children and heir to the throne. Like many Princes of Wales before him, he had an unhappy childhood, marked by a strict – sometimes brutal – regimen of learning and an emotionally crippling lack of parental affection.

At Richmond Lodge and Kew Palace, with younger brother Frederick as his sole companion, he was coached exhaustively in classics, religion, government, philosophy, history, agriculture, singing, music, fencing, boxing and horsemanship. One of his mother's attendants remembered him as 'a fine boy' with 'an open countenance, a manly air...he possessed the most obliging politeness, such as can only spring from

goodness of heart'.

He was a good-looking boy, too. In a letter to one of his sister's attendants, he describes himself as 'rather above the common size, his limbs well proportioned, and upon the whole well made, though rather too great a penchant to grow fat... I forgot to add my uggly [sic] ears. As hair is generally looked upon as a beauty, he has more hair than usually falls to everyone's share.' But George harboured a growing resentment against his father, which soon exploded in spectacular acts of youthful rebellion.

The Prince rebels

From the age of 16, he embarked on a routine of debauchery every bit as rigorous as his formal education had been, aided by the connivance of his notoriously dissolute uncles. The King was horrified but largely powerless in the face of the Prince's cunning in creating opportunities to exercise his new-found fondness for drinking, gambling and womanizing. When he took a shine to the wife of one of the Royal grooms, for instance, he simply arranged for her husband to wait on him so that his wife might appear in the Royal apartments without undue comment.

After numerous casual conquests of this sort,

5

FIT FOR A KING

The Prince liked beautiful surroundings and made it his mission in life to turn Carlton House into a palace of unparalleled magnificence. To this end he employed the architect Henry Holland to refurbish the interior with no regard for cost. An imposing hall decorated with Ionic columns of brown marble led to a graceful double staircase and the state apartments above, where the Prince would entertain guests as he lay in bed in the morning. Craftsmen were brought over from France, and paintings by English, Dutch and Flemish masters, notably Van Dyck, were bought to decorate the walls.

In March 1784, when the first stages of the alterations were complete, the Prince held a grand ball by way of a house-warming. Nine marquees were erected in the gardens, and four bands played for the guests. Over the next 30 years, the Prince lavished extraordinary amounts of money on such additions as the Chinese salon and the Gothic conservatory. Carlton House became the focus of the fashionable world while George was Prince of Wales and he swiftly ran up a debt of over half a million pounds to pay for it. But when he became King in 1820 and inherited Buckingham Palace and Windsor Castle, George had no further use for Carlton House. In 1826 he gave permission for it to be dismantled and sold piecemeal, and the finest house in London vanished as though it had never been

Mansell

the Prince fell in love for the first time in the spring of 1779, with Mary Hamilton, one of his sister's attendants. He wrote to Mary almost every day, declaring a love 'beyond the idea of everything that is human' and sending her a locket containing a lock of his hair.

But after a few months, his correspondence with Mary Hamilton abruptly ceased. The Prince had fallen in love with someone else. Mary Robinson, an actress who had spent some time in prison for debt, was one of the most desirable and notorious women of her day. On 3 December 1779 at Drury Lane, she played Perdita in a royal command performance of Shakespeare's *The Winter's Tale* attended by the Prince. He was instantly captivated.

Perdita and the Prince

The romance between 'Perdita' and 'Florizel' (Perdita's lover in the play), as the Prince called himself in his letters to her, was the *cause célèbre* of that winter of 1779-80. He promised, in writing, that he would give her £20,000 when he came of age, and on the strength of this promise she gave up acting to become his mistress. But he soon tired of her, and in the end had to buy her off to prevent her from publishing his reckless letters.

All in all, it was, in the King's words, 'a shameful scrape', but typical of the Prince's imprudence when it came to matters of the heart and of money. Though the King tried to rein in the Prince, it was to little avail. Indeed, it was as

By gracious permission of HM the Queen

🖾**Left** *Prince George with his brother Frederick. George had no childhood companions outside his own family and Frederick was his closest friend. The two boys studied, rode and were even flogged together, their father being a firm believer in the rod*

Guildhall Library, London/Bridgeman

furnishing his new home. Meanwhile, his dissipated way of life plumbed new depths.

At one of a number of parties to celebrate the return of Fox to Parliament in the elections of 1784, the Prince drank so much wine that he fell flat on his face in the middle of a dance and was violently sick when he was raised from the floor. Often, after such binges, he retired to bed in a high fever, but he never considered giving up his ruinous life-style. Among his drinking cronies at this time were the actor, John Philip Kemble, who was reputed to swallow wine by 'pailfuls', and the playwright, Richard Brinsley Sheridan.

By the summer of 1784, relations between the Prince of Wales and the King had hit rock bottom. In a letter to his brother, Prince Frederick, Prince George said his father was 'so excessively unkind' to him that he 'could hardly ever put up with it...sometimes not speaking to me when he sees me for three weeks together...he hates me; he always did, from seven years old. He will never be reconciled to me.'

> *'...he hates me; he always did, from seven years old. He will never be reconciled to me'*
>
> THE PRINCE OF WALES ON HIS FATHER

if the King's solemn injunctions to sober living goaded the Prince to ever greater bouts of dissipation. He proceeded to have affairs with a divorcee called Mrs Elliot, Lady Augusta Campbell, Lady Melbourne (who was said to have had his child), a singer called Elizabeth Billington, the Countess of Salisbury, and the Countess von Hardenburg, with whom he narrowly escaped eloping to the Continent.

The Carlton House set

His choice of male companions, too, left much to be desired as far as the King was concerned. In particular George III objected to his son's association with prominent Whig politician Charles James Fox, a formidable and vigorous opponent of the Tories and a hard-drinking gambler who had a habit of taking over the Prince's discarded mistresses, including 'Perdita' Robinson. As the Prince's 21st birthday approached, it was Fox who secured for him a substantial personal income befitting his status as heir to the throne, despite the reservations of the King who believed his son incapable of handling large sums of money wisely.

These fears were soon borne out. As another part of his coming-of-age settlement, the Prince was given his own residence, Carlton House in Pall Mall, on the understanding that he would pay for its maintenance out of his own pocket. Oblivious of his mounting debts, he poured staggering amounts of money into decorating and

👑**Right** *Mrs Mary Robinson or 'Perdita', as she was always known, received £5000 from secret service funds in return for the reckless letters written to her by the Prince of Wales, as well as an annual pension of £500 from the Prince's own income*

By gracious permission of HM the Queen

Family Album

Left *George's German mother, Queen Charlotte, in a sumptuous gown with some of the regalia of her reign displayed behind her. Thirteen of her children are grouped in the background, in front of a view of Windsor Castle*

Queen Charlotte seated at her dressing-table right with her two eldest sons, George and Frederick. The boys are both dressed in elaborate costume: Frederick's is oriental, while George is dressed as a Roman warrior, with a helmet decorated with the Prince of Wales's feathers. This love of dressing up was something that George would cultivate as he grew older. Even when he became King he retained his extravagant passion for adorning himself with fine clothes and full-dress uniforms, and throughout his life he was considered one of the arbiters of fashion

Prince George with his younger brother Frederick, the Duke of York, in the Second Drawing-Room of Buckingham Palace in 1765 right. As Frederick and George were born only a year apart, and because they spent most of their early years in each other's company, they became very close friends. The boys studied together eight hours each day, learned to fence and ride together, and were encouraged by their father to cultivate a garden plot at Kew. The brothers would remain inseparable until Frederick was sent to Hanover in Germany in 1780 to complete his military education

♛ *George was particularly fond of his three eldest sisters, Charlotte, Augusta and Elizabeth, and in 1784 he specially commissioned Gainsborough to paint this portrait right to hang at Carlton House. George was the first of George III and Queen Charlotte's 15 children, all of whom were raised with the best of intentions under a rigid code of discipline and restrictions. This upbringing, coupled with the fact that the children had few friends outside the family, undoubtedly contributed to the intimate relationships that developed among those closest in age*

A TASTE FOR OPULENCE

The Prince of Wales was well known for his love of finery and took enormous pleasure in wearing ceremonial dress. His Coronation in 1821 gave him the opportunity to indulge in the most extravagant pageantry, and £24,000 were spent on his robes alone. State visits also provided an excuse for lavish expenditure, as George ordered complete wardrobes of military and civilian dress, jewels and accessories. Uniforms delighted him; he was very knowledgeable about them, and scrupulous in his adherence to correct detail

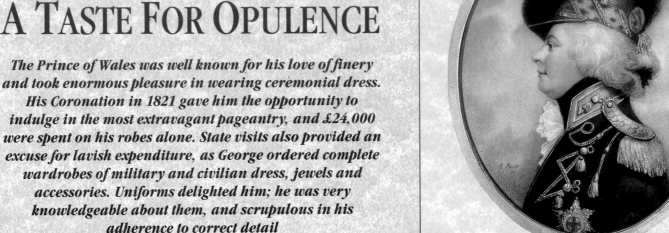

By gracious permission of HM the Queen

♔George IV is shown wearing his crimson Coronation robes *left*; the Imperial State Crown stands on the table beside him. The Collars of the Golden Fleece, the Guelphic Order, the Order of the Bath and the Order of the Garter hang from his shoulders, and the Garter itself, with the motto *Honi soit qui mal y pense*, is worn below the knee

♔The Prince was a keen follower of military affairs and loved being portrayed in army dress. This miniature, painted in 1793, shows him in the picturesque uniform of the 10th Light Dragoons, one of his favourite regiments *above*

Guildhall Library, London/Bridgeman

By gracious permission of HM the Queen

♔In this popular engraving *above* commemorating the Coronation of George IV, the King wears the Royal Robes and a Cap of Estate. His 27-foot train is borne by eight eldest sons of peers of the Realm and his path is strewn with herbs and flowers

♔When this portrait *right* was painted, the Prince was not yet a member of the army, and he is shown wearing fancy military dress rather than an actual uniform. Resting on the table are the Crown and Collar of the Order of the Garter, and the Mantle of the Garter is draped behind him. On his left breast he wears the diamond-set Garter Star

THE PURSUIT

A CHANCE VISIT TO THE OPERA WAS THE BEGINNING OF AN OVERWHELMING INFATUATION, AND THE PRINCE OF WALES SOON SHOWED HE WOULD GO TO EXTRAORDINARY LENGTHS TO ACHIEVE HIS HEART'S DESIRE

♔ *When the Prince of Wales first met Mrs Fitzherbert* above right, *she was 28 and a noted beauty. Her fine features and charm had already won the hearts of several hopeful admirers*

♔ *In his prime, the Prince of Wales cut a dashing figure. This portrait* left, *which was painted for the Royal Society of Kentish Bowmen of which the Prince was Patron and President, emphasizes his sporting prowess. He is dressed in the green uniform of the Bowmen, and leans against a statue of Diana, the mythical huntress*

I T WAS IN THE SUMMER OF 1784, WHEN HIS DEBTS were completely out of hand and his relations with his father had reached their lowest ever point, that the Prince decided one night to cast his cares aside and visit the opera. As the audience was leaving, his eye was caught by a beautiful and mysterious woman on the arm of Henry Errington, one of his acquaintances. When the Prince stepped forward to enquire who she was, Errington introduced her as his niece, the widowed Mrs Fitzherbert.

In his long and varied love life, the Prince had fallen in love at first sight many times, but his previous affairs were mere dalliances in comparison with this giddy intoxication. Formidably equipped and adept in the art of seduction, he wasted no time in turning the full force of his powers on the vision of loveliness he had spied at the opera. He followed her and sent her plaintive notes and letters by the day – sometimes by the hour. He even went so far as to inform society hostesses that he would not attend their functions unless she too were invited.

A cool reception

Mrs Fitzherbert was naturally flattered by these attentions, but she refused to take them seriously. Politely, with maddening inscrutibility, she parried the Prince's advances, knowing that her religion put marriage out of the question, and unwilling under any circumstances to compromise her virtue by becoming his mistress. But far from quenching his ardour, her coolness only inflamed it. For the first time the Prince had met a woman apparently immune to the combined power of his status, wealth and charm, and he

THE FIRST SIGHTING

Although the Prince and Mrs Fitzherbert first met and – for the Prince's part at least – fell in love in the romantic setting of the Theatre Royal, Covent Garden, it seems likely that they had seen each other on one or more occasions prior to that. Mrs Fitzherbert herself is quoted as saying that the first time was in 1780 when her second husband was still alive. They were driving in Park Lane when Thomas Fitzherbert pointed out the Prince in another carriage. A few days later, when she was driving down Park Lane to visit a friend, she noticed that the Prince was following her. She told her husband and they laughed off the incident. According to another story, they also saw each other on the banks of the Thames at Richmond in 1783, after Maria had returned from France but before she moved up to Park Street. London society was a small world in those days, and it is certainly conceivable that such sightings took place, even if they left no impression at the time

would not rest until he had devised a way of breaking her resolve.

In the end, he resorted to the sort of underhand tactics appropriate to the lurid popular melodramas of the day. One morning in November, when it was made known to him that Mrs Fitzherbert was planning to flee to the Continent to escape his increasingly desperate and hysterical entreaties, he staged a suicide attempt. Four members of his household – Lord Southampton, Lord Onslow, Edward Bouverie and Thomas Keate, the Prince's surgeon – were dispatched to her house in Park Street to tell her that he had tried to kill himself, and that he would do so again unless she agreed to see him.

The Prince in danger

She refused to go at first, suspecting – quite rightly – that it was some sort of trick, telling the four messengers 'that nothing would induce her to enter Carlton House'. But they succeeded in persuading her that the Prince's life was in real and imminent danger, and so she agreed to see him, provided she was accompanied by a chaperone. The Duchess of Devonshire said she was willing to play this role.

The Prince was in his private apartment on the ground floor, overlooking St James's Park. He was covered in blood, apparently from a wound in his side, and very pale – a picture of lovelorn

Front View of the Prince of Orange's House

🜚 *During her stay in the Hague above, Mrs Fitzherbert befriended Princess Louisa of Orange, who hoped to marry the Prince of Wales. Unaware of the irony, she asked Maria whether she thought he would make a good husband*

desperation. He told Mrs Fitzherbert he had stabbed himself with his sword. The sight of him lying there certainly had the desired effect. Shocked, frightened, 'deprived almost of consciousness', Mrs Fitzherbert was ready to do anything that would prevent the Prince making another attempt on his life. When he vowed that

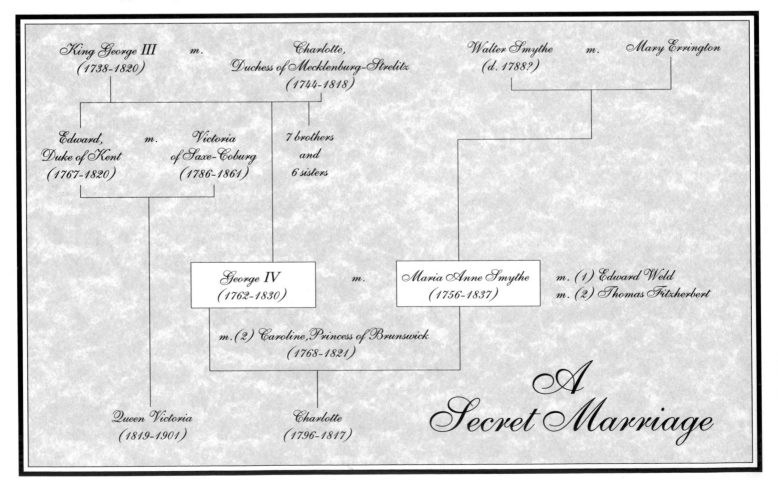

King George III (1738-1820) m. Charlotte, Duchess of Mecklenburg-Strelitz (1744-1818)

Walter Smythe (d. 1788?) m. Mary Errington

Edward, Duke of Kent (1767-1820) m. Victoria of Saxe-Coburg (1786-1861)

7 brothers and 6 sisters

George IV (1762-1830) m. Maria Anne Smythe (1756-1837) m. (1) Edward Weld m. (2) Thomas Fitzherbert

m. (2) Caroline, Princess of Brunswick (1768-1821)

Queen Victoria (1819-1901)

Charlotte (1796-1817)

A Secret Marriage

Wood, near the Hague.

♔ *Mrs Fitzherbert's friend Lady Anne Lindsay* right, *who accompanied her on her flight through Europe, had to put up with Maria's erratic moods and her frequent quarrels with her French maid*

♔ *The King was unhappy about the Prince of Wales's predilection for dancing and masquerades, but all attempts to prevent him attending these events proved futile. George was a dedicated pleasure lover who was not prepared to let parental authority stand in his way, and he often frequented public places such as Vauxhall Gardens* below

'nothing would induce him to live unless she promised to become his wife, and permitted him to put a ring round her finger', she readily gave her promise. The Duchess of Devonshire offered her own ring. The Prince placed it on Mrs Fitzherbert's finger. They were betrothed at last.

Back in her house in Park Street, Mrs Fitzherbert recovered her composure and determined not to honour a pledge made in such overwrought circumstances. She drafted a letter to the Prince in which she told him that as far as she was concerned, 'promises obtain'd in such a manner are entirely void.' Then she started packing. The next day, accompanied by her friend, Lady Anne Lindsay, she set sail for France, hoping that George would forget her and shift his notoriously fickle attentions elsewhere.

The flight to Europe

She went first to Paris, where it was not long before she received the first of a deluge of anguished letters from the Prince. After Paris, she went on to Aix-la-Chapelle, where the Prince's letters began to rain on her thick and fast. Indeed, so numerous and active were the Prince's messengers in France that French officials thought at first that Mrs Fitzherbert must be engaged on some sort of spying mission.

The letters were accurate reflections of the Prince's state of mind. The King, who knew nothing of the dramatic 'deathbed' marriage vow, but realized his son was once more in the throes of a violent and ill-advised love affair, had refused him permission to follow Mrs Fitzherbert to Europe. Writing the letters was the Prince's only safety valve, and when he was not writing them – according to Fox's mistress, Mrs Armistead – 'he cried by the hour...rolling on the

Hulton Picture Company

British Libary

Mansell

SHOWERED WITH LOVE

The love letters with which the Prince bombarded Mrs Fitzherbert during her year abroad were notable not just for their intensity and eloquence, but for their frequency and inordinate length. How many he wrote is unclear – it was probably more than a hundred – but it is known that the first ran to 18 pages and the last to 42, so it may be presumed that those in between were similarly lengthy. In them, among many terms of endearment, he addressed her as 'dearest wife', 'adored wife', and 'dearest and only belov'd Maria', calling himself her lover and her husband, 'titles [he] would not exchange for the possessions of the whole universe'. In one epistle – 37 pages long – he assured her, incredibly, that his father would agree to the union. The last letter, written on 3 November 1785 in reply to Maria's final agreement to be his wife, is the only one that survives in its entirety, and its 42 pages are ample illustration of the Prince's persuasive, flattering and fluent writing skills. He signs off with a flourish, 'Come then, oh come, dearest of Wives, best and most sacred of women, come and for ever crown with bliss, him who through Life will endeavour to convince you by his love and attention of his wishes to be the best of husbands and who will ever remain unto the latest moments of his existence unalterably Thine'

♛ *Although the precise details of Mrs Fitzherbert's voyage through Europe are not known, she probably travelled in the stage-coaches or diligences that followed set routes across the Continent below. Even the well-to-do journeyed this way, although it was arduous and not always comfortable*

Louvre, Paris/©RMN

floor, striking his forehead, tearing his hair, falling into hysterics, and swearing that he would abandon the country, forfeit the crown, sell his jewels and plate, and scrape together a competence to fly with the object of his affections to America.'

In her self-imposed exile, Mrs Fitzherbert was beginning to feel the pressure too. Her companion, Lady Anne Lindsay, described her as 'irresolute and inconsequent for much of the time'. She was stressed and confused, moving from place to place, in her own words, 'to fight off a situation which threatened to ruin my peace and happiness'.

From Aix she travelled to the Hague, carrying letters of introduction to the Court of Orange, where nothing was known of her association with the Prince of Wales. From there she moved on to Switzerland – where she met the King's brother, the Duke of Gloucester – and back to France, where she finally settled at Plombières. But try as she might, she could not shake off the attentions of the Prince. She also had to contend with the opinions of the Prince's personal and political friends back in England. Fearing for the Prince's sanity they hinted to her through emissaries that they would hold her responsible should he be driven to suicide, and advised her to settle the matter by agreeing to become his mistress. Though they succeeded in extracting a written promise from her 'that she would never marry an other person', the larger question remained unresolved.

Mrs Fitzherbert's dilemma

The psychological pressures on Mrs Fitzherbert were becoming intolerable. She had staked her life on never compromising her religion. She could not, in conscience, bring herself to be the mistress of anyone, not even the heir to the throne of England. She could only give herself body and soul to a man through the institution of marriage, yet that path too was barred to her by virtue of her Catholicism.

In the end, it seems that Mrs Fitzherbert was

Marsell

National Portrait Gallery, London

♕ *The Prince called Mrs Fitzherbert* *left his 'White Rose', partly on account of her Jacobite ancestry, and partly in tribute to her flawless complexion and innate purity*

♕ *A lifelong friend of the Prince of Wales, the Whig politician Charles James Fox* *below did all he could to dissuade George from marrying Mrs Fitzherbert. In the end the Prince was forced to lie to him about his intentions – and Fox was eventually misled into denying all knowledge of the wedding in Parliament*

the Prince of the dangers of marrying Mrs Fitzherbert, citing the country's old prejudice against Catholics and raising the possibility that the King might disinherit him. 'Make yourself easy, my dear friend', the Prince wrote in reply. 'Believe me, the world will soon be convinced that there not only is [sic] but never was, any ground for these reports.'

The Prince was not to be thwarted at this late stage, even if it meant lying through his teeth to one of his most loyal and trusted friends. In any case, he had a more pressing and distracting matter on his mind – the imminent arrival in England of his beloved Maria after more than a year out of his sight. The time and circumstances of their meeting are not documented, but the Prince anticipated the moment lingeringly in the last letter he wrote her before her return: 'I then shall either meet you in a Hackney Chaise by myself between Rochester and London, or wait till I hear of your arrival in Park Street, to which place I shall fly upon the Wings of Love the moment I know you are come...'

'...*I have told him I will be his. I know I injure him and perhaps destroy forever my own tranquility*'

MRS FITZHERBERT TO ANNE LINDSAY

simply worn into submission. In October 1785, after receiving the last of numerous suicide threats from the Prince, she wrote back to him that she was prepared to consider marriage.

Delirious with happiness, the Prince made arrangements for her homecoming. Utmost secrecy was the key element in the Prince's plan, but discretion was never his strong point. The Prince's politician friend, Charles James Fox, got wind of it even as Mrs Fitzherbert was setting sail for Dover. In a long, pleading letter, Fox warned

AN ERA OF ELEGANCE

The Prince of Wales and Maria Fitzherbert were a handsome couple and the picturesque dress of the late 18th century admirably set off their good looks, as well as allowing George to give full rein to his love of luxury and elegance. The Prince gave painstaking care to his appearance on all occasions throughout his life, and later became a central figure of the Regency 'Dandy Set' whose taste and attention to detail were to transform men's costume

Lynne Robinson

Plaid (a long piece of twilled wool cloth) worn crosswise from left shoulder to right hip, underneath belt.

Single ostrich feather plume decorates either side of this hat

Scabbard with cairngorm pommel contains two smaller dirks (long daggers) also set with cairngorms (wine-coloured semi-precious stone found on the mountains of Scotland)

♛ *Above* A typical hat of the period was high crowned, with a wide brim turned up at one side and ostrich feather trimming. Unless a wig was worn, hair would be curled and often powdered

♛ In 1822, George wore full Highland dress for his first levee as King at Holyroodhouse *left*. The three eagle's feathers in his bonnet are the mark of a chieftain and his jacket, shoulder plaid and kilt are of the Royal tartan. As well as the customary pistols, powder horn, dirk and sporran, the King wore the Orders of the Fleece, Thistle and Garter

♛*Right* The robes of the Garter. The mantle is of blue velvet lined with white taffeta, with a crimson velvet hood and the Garter badge embroidered on the left side. A crimson velvet surcoat is worn underneath. The 'Great George', a heavy gold and enamel badge of St George slaying the dragon, hangs from a gold neck chain. The eight-pointed star and 'Lesser George' hang from the right hip and the hat is of black velvet with a plume of white ostrich feathers and a single black heron feather

Base of beaver fur hat trimmed with contrast braid and jewels

Tall military hat trimmed with ostrich feather plumes

Christie's Colour Library

♛The tall hat of beaver fur *left* with an ostrich-feather plume was part of the Hussar's uniform. Military styles influenced George's taste and it was he who introduced the fashion for high collars and cravats

The classical lines of the Empire style gave way to more elaborate draping in women's dress *below* but white remained a popular colour. The waist went back to its natural position – resulting in the return of the corset – and skirts became fuller, with flounces or scalloped edges on the petticoat or overskirt. Appliqué trimming continued to be used on bodice, sleeves and skirt

Maria's ivory fan *above* was a gift from George. The delicate fretwork shafts, so thin as to be translucent, are held together by a diamond-headed rivet

Mansell

Sachet in three sections embroidered with a flower pattern in gold thread

Cornflower pattern stamped on the outside of sachet

Inside of sachet lined with cream-coloured satin

Satin sachets for protecting valuable or delicate items were very popular. Maria embroidered one for carrying a purse *far left* when she was 75. She used another sachet *left* to keep her handkerchief in

♕*Right* Tall-crowned hats with wide brims were as popular for women as for men. This one tied under the chin with a thin scarf

Hair piled high on the head and decorated with ostrich plumes, jewels and flowers, a short train falling from the back of head-dress

Dress has a closely fitted bodice with lightly fitting set-in sleeves

Skirt of this gown draped and gathered. Trimmed with braids and fringing

The tulip shape of this skirt was probably achieved with the use of layers of starched petticoats

♕Gillray's cartoon of the wedding shows Maria in a gown with the low neckline correct for court or evening-dress combined with an elaborate headdress of flowers, lace and plumes *left*. Maria had no need to add artificial tresses, and was famous for not powdering her hair

♕For her portrait by Gainsborough *below* Maria wore informal day dress, with her hair drawn back softly from her face and little jewellery

Thomas Gainsborough: Mrs Fitzherbert. The Fine Arts Museums of San Francisco, Mildred Anna Williams Collection

MARRIED IN SECRET

THE PRINCE AND MRS FITZHERBERT, AWARE OF THE DANGERS, PROCEEDED WITH THE WEDDING, BUT SOON THE COUPLE FOUND THEMSELVES EMBROILED IN AN ELABORATE DECEPTION

MRS FITZHERBERT WAS BACK IN ENGLAND. The date of the secret marriage had been fixed. But, recklessly happy as he was, the Prince knew that marrying her was a constitutional minefield. Not only would it contravene the Royal Marriage Act which declared null and void any marriage that took place without the monarch's consent. The Prince also knew that by marrying a Roman

Catholic he was defying the Act of Settlement and running the risk of forfeiting the throne.

It was imperative that he find a Church of England clergyman willing to conduct the ceremony, for before 1791 marriages – even between Catholics – were not legal if they had only been solemnized by a Catholic priest. Finding an Anglican clergyman willing to oblige, however, was no easy task, even for as influential and

♛Below *The secret marriage. The priest is statesman Edmund Burke, known at the time for his Catholic sympathies, and one of the witnesses is Sheridan, as renowned for his drinking as for his plays, with a bottle of wine in each of his coat pockets. Mrs Fitzherbert is being given away by Charles James Fox*

WIFE & no WIFE — or — A trip to the Continent.

Hulton Picture Company

Mansell

St James's Square was, when built in the second half of the 17th century, one of the most fashionable addresses in London. It gradually became less and less chic, but in George's time left it still had 'an Air of Grandeur'. St James's Palace stood nearby. Built by Henry VIII, it too had seen more popular days, and George did not much care for it, but the Palace remained the centre of court ceremonial, where occasions of state, balls and formal receptions took place. Receptions at court included what were called Drawing-Rooms below, after the rooms where they took place, and to which only the most socially desirable people were invited. Regulations about dress and behaviour were strict: one poor woman attending a reception at George's father's court complained of not being allowed to sneeze!

persuasive a figure as the Prince – officiating at such a ceremony was itself a criminal act under the terms of the Royal Marriage Act.

First of all he turned the full force of his charm on the Reverend S Johnes Knight, whom he summoned to Carlton House. The Prince was wearing his dressing-gown, which he lifted to reveal the wound in his side as physical proof of the depth and sincerity of his feelings for Mrs Fitzherbert. Many years later, Knight recalled the meeting in a letter. 'I could not bear to see him so miserable,' he wrote. 'Bear in mind I was young, and could not help being flattered by the attentions of a Prince, who was one of the best arguers, in his own cause, I have ever known.'

Knight makes his excuses

The Prince extracted a promise from Knight that he would be waiting outside Mrs Fitzherbert's house between seven and eight o'clock in the evening on the appointed day. But George's charm wove only a temporary spell. Even as he reached the street outside Carlton House, Knight was having second thoughts. Later that day he wrote to the Prince asking to be excused from his promise. The Prince was obliged to turn his attentions elsewhere, into the shadier reaches of the Anglican clergy.

The Reverend John Burt, a young curate who had spent some time in Fleet Prison for debt, was induced to perform the ceremony by a piece of shameless bribery. The Prince promised that when he became King he would make Burt a bishop. He also agreed to give him £500 to clear

'It is a very hazardous undertaking'

LADY JERNINGHAM ON THE MARRIAGE

his debts. Burt needed no time to examine his conscience. He needed only to know when and where the ceremony would take place: at dusk, on 15 December 1785, at Mrs Fitzherbert's house in Park Street. Burt was already there when the Prince walked into his bride's drawing-room at the appointed time, and the doors were locked behind him. Also in attendance, as witnesses, were Mrs Fitzherbert's uncle, Henry Errington, and her brother, John Smythe. Errington had been against the marriage at first but, bowing to the inevitable, he had agreed to

Angelo Hornak

🜲 *The title of the Gillray cartoon above, 'The April Fool or the Follies of a Night', refers to the imprudence of the secret marriage. As well as the happy couple, the print shows Edmund Burke, who plays a musical accompaniment on the fire irons, and George's friend George Hanger, who joins in the dance. With its scenes from* Hamlet *on the wall, it also makes reference to the Prince's love of the theatre*

give his niece away. Outside the door, a friend, Orlando Bridgeman, stood guard.

After the short formalities, the Prince wrote out the marriage certificate, signed it, and passed it to his new wife, Errington and Smythe to sign in turn. He then gave it to Mrs Fitzherbert – for so she would continue to call herself – for safekeeping. After the Prince's death, she deposited the certificate in the vaults of Coutts Bank, but not before cutting out the names of the witnesses to save them from possible prosecution. Her own and the Prince's signatures remain intact. Burt and the witnesses dispersed, promising to keep the secret and having the best incentive – their

own safety – to do so. The newlyweds then left immediately for a short honeymoon.

Their destination was Mrs Fitzherbert's villa at Richmond. The snow lay thick on the roads that night, and they made slow progress. At Hammersmith, their carriage broke down, and they ate dinner at an inn there before continuing their journey. The honeymoon was soon over and they were back in town before Christmas, to embark on a married life of calculated deception.

Even before their return, rumours of the marriage were spreading far and wide. Thomas Orde MP, writing to the Duke of Rutland, said, 'I am very sorry for it, for it does him infinite mis-

A F Kersting

🜲 *George and Maria spent their brief honeymoon at her villa in Richmond, Surrey, though the exact location is unknown today. But Ormeley Lodge* left *lays claim to being the house in question, and this lovely Queen Anne villa on Ham Common does feature, carved in the brick above the entrance, the Prince of Wales's feathers*

chief, particularly amongst the trading and lower sort of people, and if true must ruin him...'

Lady Jerningham, a Roman Catholic, told her daughter Charlotte, 'Mrs Fitzherbert has, I believe, been married to the Prince. But it is a very hazardous undertaking, as there are two Acts of Parliament against the validity of such an alliance...God knows how it will turn out – it may be the glory of our belief, or it may be to the great dismay and destruction of it!' Such speculation was not confined to personal correspondence or high society drawing-rooms. The scandal sheets of the day operated relatively free of legal constraint, and now they faithfully relayed the gossip and generated a fair share of their own. Prints and cartoons followed suit, many of them grossly vulgar and scurrilous. They were displayed in shop windows and sold on the streets, to the great delight of the mass of ordinary people, who found scandal involving royalty as compulsive as we do today.

The Prince knew how important it was to quell such rumours. For appearance's sake, he and Maria continued to live separately, though she moved from Park Street to a house in St James's Square to be nearer Carlton House. When they were seen in public, at a party or the opera, the Prince took care to behave with

> ### 'If ever the Prince loved any woman it was she...'
>
> MARY FRAMPTON ON MRS FITZHERBERT

extreme decorum towards her. As a mutual friend, Lady Charlotte Bury, wrote in her diary, 'The Prince never forgot to go through the form of saying to Mrs Fitzherbert, with the most respectful bow, "Madam, may I be allowed the honour of seeing you home in my carriage?"'

An awkward situation

At the same time, he made it known that any invitation extended to him must also include Mrs Fitzherbert, and that the usual forms of protocol should be waived where she was concerned – she was always to be placed at the same table as himself. It was a strange charade. Most of London knew of or strongly suspected the marriage. And the Prince and Maria were aware that it was common knowledge. Nevertheless, the pretence had to be maintained.

It also placed Mrs Fitzherbert herself in an awkward situation, though it seems that in general people behaved with great tact and warmth towards her. There were exceptions. The families of her first two husbands shunned her, as did her erstwhile friend, the celebrated hostess, Lady Sefton. But her behaviour was so impeccably modest and discreet that few people could find it in their hearts to resent her. During the early months of 1786, the Prince and Mrs

By gracious permission of HM the Queen

THE SPENDTHRIFT

The Prince never learned to curb his natural inclination to spend money with reckless extravagance. Carlton House was a constant drain on his expenses, to the 'grief and vexation' of George Hotham, his treasurer. He was spending well over £1000 a month on furnishings alone, and the annual bill for the upkeep of the stables was £31,000. The Prince also had a particular weakness for fine clothes. In one period of seven weeks or so he ordered 62 waistcoats of various sorts, from 'fancy lilac double breasted' to 'brown nankeen striped Marseilles quilted'. On another occasion, in the space of six months he bought 'ten dozen pairs of white long gloves'. His muffs, of muscovy sable, cost 100 guineas each. He spent £20 a week on toiletries alone, and ordered toothbrushes in batches of 36. He bought almost everything in ridiculously large quantities. When he needed a new walking stick, he bought 32. In 1786, when the King called him to account and demanded to know the extent of his debts, Hotham was horrified to discover that the Prince owed £269,878 – a staggering sum in those days

The MORNING after MARRIAGE ___ or ___ A scene on the Continent.

> **'I pity her for she seems modest, unaffected and unpretending but not very wise'**
>
> LADY LOUISA STUART
> ON MRS FITZHERBERT

GILLRAY'S CARICATURES

The satirical cartoons of the Prince and Mrs Fitzherbert that appeared in the newspapers following their secret marriage were for the most part crude affairs, long since consigned to obscurity. But those of James Gillray, cruel as they are, have withstood the test of time, perhaps because of their liveliness and sense of immediacy.

Gillray was the finest of London's political cartoonists. By 1786, his work was selling in large quantities – on the Continent as well as in Britain – and many people, including statesmen and politicians, dreaded his sharp wit. In that year he produced a sketch entitled 'The Morning after Marriage', in which Mrs Fitzherbert is sitting on a bed pulling on her stocking, while the Prince, leaning on a table with his garter hanging down his leg, stretches and scratches his head.

Despite Gillray's success, by 1811 he had begun to go mad and would later only retain brief intervals of sanity

Fitzherbert were rarely out of each other's sight, and most of London society came to accept them as unconditionally as if their marriage had been public and above board.

The London season that year was an unusually exuberant one, and people looked to the Prince of Wales to lead the glittering social round. Mrs Fitzherbert played hostess at many memorable occasions at Carlton House, described by a contemporary commentator as

👑 *Orlando Bridgeman* right *was one of the Prince of Wales's good friends as well as a friend of the Smythe family, one that was considered trustworthy enough to stand guard at the wedding: he was posted at the door to sound the alarm if necessary. Bridgeman was a Member of Parliament for Wigan, and in 1815 was created first Earl of Bradford*

'the centre in which genius, taste, and wit were to be found, and to which elegance, beauty, and refinement in the fair sex most amply resorted.'

Regular guests included the most notable of society beauties, the Duchesses of Cumberland and Devonshire, Lady Melbourne, Lady Clare and Mrs Sheridan, and some of the most influential men of the day, among them Fox, Sheridan and the future Prime Minister Earl Grey.

A gratifying change

Domestically, the Prince had never been happier. Those of his friends and advisers for whom his erratic behaviour and dissolute way of life had frequently been a cause of alarm in the past were gratified by the change in him. Maria was a calming, stabilizing influence, which was reason enough to welcome their association. But other aspects of the Prince's life were in as much of a mess as ever. His relationship with his father, the King, was in a state of estrangement now worsened by a frosty exchange of letters concerning his ever-present and mounting debts.

The King did not refuse point-blank to help the Prince out of his financial difficulties. But he made it clear that he was not prepared to bale him out yet again without a proper examination of the debts, and a pledge from the Prince to limit his expenditure in the future. The Prince admitted that his debts were twice what they had been two years before, but refused to give any explanation, or make any promise to curb his spending. He told the King that henceforth he would not be asking for his help because he had 'no reason to expect either at present or in future the smallest assistance from [his] Majesty'.

'I will never marry'

The King tried a different tack. Through intermediaries, it was made clear to the Prince that the King would look more kindly on his son and heir if he would consent to marry a suitable foreign princess. It seems astonishing that talk of the Prince's marriage should not have reached the ears of the King by this time, and it can only be that he chose to discount such rumours because the consequences of believing and acting upon them were too grave to contemplate. Certainly the Prince was outraged by suggestions that he contract a marriage of convenience and respectability just to keep the King happy. 'I will never marry. My resolution is taken on that subject,' he said. 'I have settled it with Frederick [his brother, the Duke of York]...Frederick will marry, and the crown will descend to his children.'

Faced with this intractability, the King refused to approve a decent allowance for the Prince that would have enabled him to manage his debts. Their disagreement had now reached a form of brinkmanship, and the Prince was not prepared to back down. He went instead for the

Christie's Colour Library

🖾 *Whether or not George discussed his marriage with his mother is a matter of conjecture, but it is certain that Maria was not received by the Queen, and some of her former friends now shunned her. But the Duchess of Devonshire, Lady Melbourne and Mrs Dawson Damer – dressed as the three witches from Macbeth in the painting above – remained loyal friends of both Maria and the Prince. Georgiana, the Duchess of Devonshire, often appeared in public with Maria, who was a frequent and honoured guest at Devonshire House. Lady Betsy Melbourne was considered one of the top hostesses of the day. She was an old flame of George's, and he was later to claim – falsely – that she died in his arms. Mrs Dawson Damer was the married name of Minney Seymour, Mrs Fitzherbert's adopted daughter, who became almost as close to George as she was to Maria*

dramatic gesture. He would close Carlton House, dismiss much of his household, sell off his carriages and horses, and not appear again in public until he was able to do so 'with that dignity and splendour' which befitted his status as heir to the throne of England.

The King interpreted this move in the way it was almost certainly intended, as a form of public martyrdom designed to highlight his apparently unreasonable behaviour towards his son. Others read into it further evidence of the Prince's growing maturity and sense of responsibility. The Duke of Cumberland told him his 'manly conduct' was 'universally approved'. Fox congratulated him on his 'manly and judicious step' which had 'united the universal opinion of all descriptions of men in his favour'.

In July 1786, having thus inadvertently created a more favourable political climate in which to enjoy to the full those early months with his secret bride, the Prince moved down to a small but increasingly fashionable resort on the Sussex coast called Brighton. There he would enjoy the sun and the sea and, above all, the invigorating company of Mrs Fitzherbert.

THE ROYAL PAVILION

When the Prince moved to Brighton House in 1786 it was a modest, double-fronted residence. But it was not long before he was planning an ambitious building programme. The earliest additions were in the Neo-Classical style, but between 1802 and 1804 Chinese taste took over the interior. Stables resembling an Indian mausoleum were built, and the main exterior was eventually remodelled along Indian lines

The architect John Nash began enlarge the Pavilion in 1815, and over the next five years transformed its exterior, adding domes, tent-shaped roofs, minarets and arched windows. The imposing East Front *below* looks out on to the lawn and the busy Steine beyond

Angelo Hornak

Angelo Hornak

👑 The Saloon *left* was the grandest reception room in the Pavilion. Remodelled in 1823, its gold and cream decorative scheme marries Oriental influence – as seen in the 'Chinese' wallpaper – with Neo-Classical restraint

👑 Some apartments in the Pavilion were reserved for members of the Royal Family; this room *above* is known as Queen Charlotte's Bedroom. Although not as lavish as the rooms used by the Dukes of Clarence and York, it is prettily decorated. The four-poster bed and Chinese-style furniture are original to the building

👑 *Left* One of four cabinets decorated with Japanese lacquer which George probably brought from Carlton House. It belongs in the South Drawing-Room, which leads out from the Banqueting Room, and was originally used as an after-dinner reception area

♛The domed ceiling with its suspended dragon and lotus-bowl chandelier dominates the splendid Banqueting Room *right*. Chinese oil paintings pasted on to dragon paper and framed with elaborate bamboo borders decorate the walls

♛The Prince loved giving banquets, and insisted on high standards of cuisine. His Great Kitchen *above* was remarkable not only for its fantasy palm-tree columns, but also because it represented the last word in convenience and technological modernity. The power for the roasting spits *above right* came from a revolving vane in the chimney

♛A mood of restrained opulence prevails in the ground-floor private apartments that George used when he became King; the decoration of the Library *right* is more conducive to quiet contemplation than riotous entertaining. The walls are hung with hand-stencilled green satin and the ceiling painted to resemble a clouded sky. The silver-gilt palm tree inkstand on the desk was a gift from Lord or Lady Conyngham

Angelo Hornak

BY THE SEA

TO GEORGE, BRIGHTON SEEMED THE IDEAL PLACE TO LIVE HIDDEN AWAY WITH MARIA, BUT HE WAS WORRIED THAT THEIR MARRIAGE WOULD BE MADE PUBLIC IN PARLIAMENT

By gracious permission of HM the Queen

♛ *George* right *was loved by his servants, who often accompanied him on his travels. Louis Weltje* below *– a pastry-chef famed for his ugliness – was the Prince's Clerk of the Kitchen, and it was he who, on the Prince's return to Brighton, was dispatched to find a house*

THE PRINCE WAS NO STRANGER TO THE civilized delights of Brighton. He had made his first visit there in September 1783, staying with his uncle and aunt, the Duke and Duchess of Cumberland. It had been exhilarating to escape the suffocating staidness of the 'usual circle of old tabbies' surrounding his parents, the King and Queen, and he had determined to return.

Having a good time
The following summer he did so, on the advice of his physicians who recommended sea-bathing as a cure for swollen glands in his throat. Apart from swimming, he had gone to the Brighton races, taken long walks along the sea front, and – allegedly at least – had several enjoyably uncomplicated affairs with local girls. The *Morning Post* reported that 'The visit of a certain gay, illustrious character at Brighton, has frightened away a number of old maids, who used constantly to frequent that place...'

Brighton and the Prince were made for each other, and he made up his mind to live there, instructing one of his attendants, Louis Weltje, to find him a house. The house Weltje chose was 'a respectable farmhouse' – the forerunner of his famous Brighton Pavilion – overlooking the sea front on the east side of the Steine, one of the city's main streets. When the Prince retired there on 11 July 1786, his financial circumstances were apparently severely straitened, for he travelled down to Brighton in a hired coach, the Brighton Dilly. A contemporary cartoon shows the coach laden with furniture, vegetables and wine, as if the Prince were a vagabond. In fact this gesture of apparent financial sacrifice was a hollow one. The prospect of a quiet, romantic summer by the seaside with his beloved Mrs Fitzherbert was a delicious one indeed.

He had to wait a day short of two weeks for Mrs Fitzherbert to join him in Brighton. Though they were now free of the prying eyes and wagging tongues of London society – another advantage of Brighton that commended itself to the Prince – they did not dare to live openly together. They could scarcely have been closer, however. Mrs Fitzherbert moved into a small villa with green shutters literally at the bottom of the Prince's garden. She also was very fond of Brighton. Over the next several years Mrs Fitzherbert and the Prince would help elevate it to one of the most fashionable resorts in Europe, flocked to by the most notable luminaries of the Georgian era.

Local hero

The Prince became something of a hero to the local people. He and Mrs Fitzherbert were often to be seen promenading arm in arm on the Steine, mixing with an unaffected familiarity with passers-by, a picture of romantic contentment. In those brief but happy months, the Prince appeared to be a reformed character. He drank only moderately, gambled hardly at all, and entertained quietly: only a few of his friends came to visit him, and those who did were the quieter ones. In a letter to the Duke of Rutland, the Earl of Mornington remarked that 'People talked much of the Prince's reform, particularly in this spot which he has chosen as the place of his retreat. Mrs Fitzherbert is here, and they say with child.'

Maria's children?

The rumour that Mrs Fitzherbert had one or more children by the Prince of Wales has been a persistent one. Certainly she never denied having had children. In 1833, when her relative, Lord Stourton, suggested that she write on the back of her marriage certificate, 'No issue from this marriage,' he said 'she smilingly objected on

Youthful as Hebe bewitching As Venus

Fine girls by Gad Bob

British Museum, London/Bridgeman

BEAUS and BELLES or a PROMENADE SCENE at BRIGHTON

the score of delicacy'. The year before she died, she wrote out a document declaring that 'I Maria Fitzherbert...testify that my union with George, Prince of Wales, was without issue,' but she could not bring herself to sign it. Among several somewhat fanciful theories, the possibility that her adopted niece, Mary Anne Smythe, was in reality her daughter by the Prince of Wales is less easy to dispose of.

Officially, Mary Anne Smythe was the illegitimate daughter of her brother, John Smythe, one of the witnesses at her secret wedding, but according to family records he did not have any children. She married Edward Stafford Jerningham, brother of Lord Stafford. Her grandson, also a Lord Stafford, said there was 'strong

By the time George made his first visit to Brighton, the town was already a fashionable seaside resort, as popular for the pretty young women of doubtful virtue who flocked there above as for the supposedly beneficial results of sea bathing. While George must have looked forward to strolling along the sea front, he may well have dreaded the journey from London: even though he travelled in a post-chaise rather than the more common public stage-coach with 'company of every description' below, it would still have taken the best part of a day

Mansell

'LONDON BY THE SEA'

At the turn of the 18th century, the Sussex seaside town of Brighton was a small fishing port called Brighthelmstone with a scattering of inhabitants. One hundred years later, its population had risen to more than 7000 and the *Brighton Directory* – admittedly a partial witness – was proclaiming it 'the most frequented [and] without exception one of the most fashionable towns in the Kingdom'. Dominating the sea front was the Prince's extraordinary Pavilion. The classic and elegant Royal Crescent had just been completed, and people from London were buying property there in increasingly large numbers. Brighton first gained in popularity through the supposed efficacy of its sea water in curing various ailments, but it was the Royal connection – and in particular the patronage of the future George IV – that really put the town on the map. Its invigorating air, large sweep of beach (supervised by Martha Gunn, the 'bathing-woman of Brighton' *right*, who assisted all the most fashionable lady bathers, including Maria), cliff-top walks and unhurried pace of life were an obvious balm to the fetid and grimy streets of Georgian London and the hurly-burly of that city's political and social life. Because its population had largely been displaced from the capital, Brighton became known as 'London by the Sea', a tag that sticks to this day

Victoria and Albert Museum, London/Bridgeman

'*The fact not only never could have happened legally, but never did happen in any way whatsoever*'

CHARLES JAMES FOX ON THE MARRIAGE

circumstantial evidence' to support the family belief that his great grandparents were indeed the future George IV and Mrs Fitzherbert.

There were other rumours: that Mrs Fitzherbert gave birth to a boy in France in 1793, and that there was another son, brought up as his own by the Prince's friend, Sir James Harris. Mrs Fitzherbert's adopted daughter, Mary 'Minney' Seymour, daughter of Lord Hugh and Lady Horatia Seymour, said late in her life that Mrs Fitzherbert had more than one child by the Prince. But there are no such references in any of the Royal Archives, and any evidence there may have been in Mrs Fitzherbert's private papers has been destroyed.

Certainly, if she were pregnant during 1786, she would have had a reasonable opportunity of keeping the confinement secret, for she and the Prince lived extremely privately, and began to move about among various borrowed houses – including the Duke of Gloucester's at Bagshot and Lord North's at Bushey – as autumn drew on and the summer bloom of Brighton faded.

The same old problem

After one of the happiest and most tranquil periods that the Prince would ever enjoy, the old problem of money was reasserting itself. His continued estrangement from the King made any private family settlement impossible. Though the King and Queen had heard good reports of the Prince's reformed behaviour, the King still stubbornly refused to heal the rift between them. In August 1786, when a madwoman, Mary Nicholson, tried to stab the King as he stepped from his carriage, the Prince hurried off to Windsor to express his filial concern and loyalty. But the King refused to see him. After this episode, the Prince knew he had no option but to turn to Parliament for the settlement he sorely needed to pay his debts.

George's desperation

The Prince did not do so blindly. He knew that if his affairs became the subject of parliamentary debate, there was a real risk that his marriage to Mrs Fitzherbert would become a matter of public knowledge. Fox was horrified. It would be disastrous if the staunchly Protestant British public were to learn that the Whig opposition had been supporting the claims of a man who had contracted a secret marriage with a Roman Catholic. But the Prince was now desperate. If Fox and the Whigs would not raise the matter on his behalf, he would find an independent MP who would.

On 20 April 1787, Nathaniel Newman, Member for the City of London, rose to his feet in the House to do the Prince's bidding, asking 'whether it was the design of Ministers to bring forward any proposition to rescue the Prince of

Wales from his present very embarrassed situation'. Prime Minister William Pitt replied that it was for the King alone to raise such a matter, but Newman would not be deflected from his purpose. He said he would ask the question again in a few days, on 4 May.

Bluff and counter-bluff

A game of bluff and counter-bluff was now under way. Wishing to limit the damage, Pitt raised the matter himself four days later, warning that if Newman persevered with his motion, it might lead 'to the disclosure of circumstances which he should otherwise think it his duty to conceal'. Sheridan then spoke up in defence of the Prince, suggesting that such insinuations should not go unanswered. As one member put it, 'The fat was now in the fire.'

Over the next few days, Fox, Sheridan and the Prince held frantic talks on the best course of action – to deny the marriage, and run the risk of being publicly exposed and humiliated, or to admit it and face political ruin and – conceivably – worse. Sheridan also discussed the matter with

♛ In 1786, the Prince heard news that his father, George III right, had been stabbed. He immediately rushed off to Windsor, but his father refused to see him, even though he was in the next room. The King loved Windsor Castle below, although for the first half of his 40-year-long association with the place he and his family actually lived in Queen's Lodge, a house opposite the south front. Meanwhile, King George supervised a programme of repair and restoration of the Castle, and in 1805 there was a great housewarming party to celebrate the family's reoccupation of the Castle's Royal apartments. The King was to end his years at Windsor, in a lonely suite far from the apartments of the rest of his family. George IV later decided to redesign much of the Castle, and in so doing destroyed Queen's Lodge, which was in the way

Mrs Fitzherbert, whose future was now also in the balance. He did not say outright that she might have to suffer the shame of a public denial that the marriage had taken place, but he impressed upon her just how dangerous was the Prince's position. Mrs Fitzherbert told him she was 'like a dog with a log tied round its neck'. They 'must protect' her.

Fox decided to bluff it out. On 30 April, to a packed and tense House, he rose to repudiate the 'miserable calumny', the 'monstrous report of a fact which had not the smallest degree of foundation'. Piling on the indignation, he described the rumour of marriage as a 'low malicious falsehood', a 'tale in every particular unfounded...The fact not only never could have happened legally, but never did happen in any way whatsoever.' When he finally sat down, he felt he had made himself clear.

Immediately after this performance, Fox felt tremendous relief that the matter had been laid to rest, for the time being at least, and that he had taken the best possible course of action in the

Richard Brinsley Sheridan right was a great favourite of the Prince, especially during the early years of his relationship with Maria. Best known as the dramatist who produced such comic masterpieces as The Rivals (which was written when he was only 23) and The School for Scandal, he was also an MP for more than 30 years. Though he was a brilliant speaker, his career in Parliament was not successful, and he was to die in poverty in 1816. In Gillray's cartoon below, an allusion to a scandalous story current at the time that seems to have had no basis in reality, Sheridan is caressing Mrs Fitzherbert while the Prince, unaware of what is going on behind his back, plays with a 'bandalure', one of the fashionable playthings of the day used for whiling away time

BANDELURES.

thus sits the Dupe, content!
Pleases himself with Toys, thinks Heav'n secure.
Depends on Woman's smiles, & thinks the Man
His Soul is wrapt in, can be nought but true;

London Pub d. Feb y. 28. 1791, by S.W. Fores, No. 3 Piccadilly.

Fond Fool, arouse! shake off thy childish Dream,
Behold Love's falshood, Friendships perjur'd troth;
Nor sit & sleep, for all around the World
Thy shame is known, while thou alone art blind.

Blackmore

Mansell

circumstances. Shortly afterwards, however, he ran into Orlando Bridgeman, who said to him, 'Mr Fox, I hear that you have denied in the House the Prince's marriage to Mrs Fitzherbert. You have been misinformed. I was at the marriage.' Thereafter, Fox became increasingly concerned that his falsehood would be exposed, and for a year afterwards he avoided situations where he might meet the Prince.

The day after Fox had made his statement in the House, the Prince visited Mrs Fitzherbert in Park Street. He found her 'in an agony of tears', 'deeply afflicted and furious against Fox'. According to one report, he said to her, 'Only conceive, Maria, what Fox did yesterday. He went down to the House and denied that you and I were man and wife! Did you ever hear of such a thing?' Lady Anne Lindsay recalled that Maria 'burst into tears, said that she had indeed been shamefully used, that the Prince had been "like a mad thing" at the liberty Fox had taken'. To another friend she complained that Fox had 'rolled her in the kennel like a street walker'.

Sheridan to the rescue

Mrs Fitzherbert was so furious that she threatened to break off relations with the Prince and refused to see him. He realized that somehow he must seek to undo the damage to her virtue and integrity that Fox had caused by his denial. He called on his loyal friend, Sheridan, to attempt the unenviable task of rehabilitating Mrs Fitzherbert's good name without admitting the fact of the marriage.

On 4 May, Sheridan delivered to the House a speech of cunning equivocation in which he referred to Mrs Fitzherbert as 'another whose character claimed, and was entitled, to the truest and most general respect'. The listening Members seemed satisfied, though several could not forbear to smirk when Sheridan described Mrs Fitzherbert's situation as 'truly respectable' after Fox had so recently made it clear that she was the Prince's mistress.

Bad old ways

But if the Prince expected Mrs Fitzherbert to forgive and forget the humiliation, he was mistaken. She still refused to see him, and as the days wore on and she showed no sign of softening towards him, he fell into his bad old ways, working himself up into a violent fever and drinking excessively. At a ball given by Lady Hopetoun, he arrived so drunk he could hardly stand up. But after a bottle and a half of champagne had revived him, he 'posted himself in the doorway, to the terror of everybody that went by, flung his arms round the Duchess of Ancaster's neck and kissed her with a great *smack*, threatened to pull Lord Galloway's wig off and knock out his false teeth, and played all the pranks of a drunken man

---

'Poor Mrs Fitzherbert is very much to be pitied'

MRS SHERIDAN

---

upon the stage, till some of his companions called for his carriage, and almost forced him away'. Shortly afterwards, he threatened to kill himself.

Mrs Fitzherbert, meanwhile, to her great surprise, was as popular and welcome as ever in London society, and it was this fact as much as any sympathy she felt for the Prince's position that persuaded her to relax her attitude towards him. Their reconciliation took place at a ball given by the Duchess of Gordon, where they were seen dancing closely together. It had been a terrible few months, but now the Prince's finances were sorted out, the King and Queen welcomed him at Windsor and, most importantly, his beloved Maria Fitzherbert was once more folded in his arms.

THE BALANCE OF POWER

George IV and his father George III reigned against a background of uneasy parliamentary balance. Robert Walpole, who became Britain's first Prime Minister in 1721, was a Whig, but the Tories – traditionally the party of the squires and parsons – gained control of the government in 1783 during the reign of George III and held the balance of power almost continuously until George IV's death in 1830. During this period William Pitt (shown *below* addressing the House of Commons on the French declaration of war in 1793) was twice appointed Prime Minister.

The Whig Party – the forerunner of the Liberal Party – drew its support mainly from the merchant and business classes. As Prince of Wales, the future George IV was a staunch supporter of the Whigs, among whom he numbered some of his best friends, including Fox and Sheridan. His parents, George III and Queen Charlotte, on the other hand, were firm Tories, and therein lay the root of much of the bad feeling between George III and his successor. This came to a head during the Regency crisis of 1789, when the Queen believed the Prince was siding with the Whigs to overthrow the Tories

National Portrait Gallery, London

SHARED SECRETS

Although the marriage of George, the Prince of Wales and Maria Fitzherbert was – more or less – public knowledge, it was never officially confirmed. As a result, a certain amount of secrecy and discretion had to be maintained throughout their lives. Nevertheless, tokens of their love and the happy times they spent together still exist

Mansell

♛*Left* This locket contains a miniature painting of the eye of Mrs Fitzherbert. One of a pair – the other locket enclosed a painting of George's eye – it is a bizarre token of their affair

♛*Below* The couple spent many happy days in Mrs Fitzherbert's modest but comfortable house in Brighton, known as Steine House, which was conveniently placed near the Pavilion. Maria was happiest in Brighton, where she was fondly regarded by the local people

♛A romantic stipple engraving of Maria Fitzherbert *right*. Below her image is a symbolic testament of George's love: the Royal plumes pierced by an arrow

Mrs Fitzherbert

National Portrait Gallery, London

Ray Leaning

♛One of the more elaborate of Mrs Fitzherbert's personal keepsakes was an exquisitely carved ivory fan *below right* which features a miniature of her husband George as the young Prince of Wales, painted by Richard Cosway

Mansell

AN ABIDING LOVE

**THE LOVE THE PRINCE FELT FOR MRS FITZHERBERT WAS
PROFOUND AND ENDURING, SURVIVING POLITICAL CRISES,
INFIDELITIES AND A FINAL PERIOD OF ESTRANGEMENT**

THE PRINCE'S ASSOCIATION WITH MRS Fitzherbert had endured its worst crisis so far, and the experience of nearly losing her seemed to jolt him into a new sense of his responsibilities towards her. He began to treat her as if she were indeed the legally constituted Princess of Wales, showering her with gifts and setting her up in great splendour in an expensively furnished house near his own in Pall Mall.

Immediately after their reunion, on 6 July 1787, Mrs Fitzherbert and the Prince returned to Brighton for another summer by the sea. The Prince's original house on the Steine had now been replaced by the first version of that remarkable architectural extravaganza, the Brighton Pavilion. George seems to have been supremely contented during those summer months. His finances were now in order, Mrs Fitzherbert was living close by, and the Pavilion – even before the addition of those famous onion-shaped domes – was a sanctuary of fantasy and opulence.

The King's madness

But another constitutional crisis was looming. In October, the Prince received word that his father had fallen ill. Over the following months the King's condition deteriorated nearly to the point of death. It is now thought that he was almost certainly suffering from porphyria, a rare and terrible hereditary disorder of the metabolism which produces symptoms of hysteria, paranoia and schizophrenia.

While a succession of physicians fought to contain the illness, it appeared increasingly likely that the Prince would assume the role of

Regent for the duration of the King's incapacity. A fierce political power struggle developed behind the scenes. Ranged on one side were the Tories, led by Prime Minister Pitt and supported by the Queen, who feared the Prince would oust them from power, on the other the Whigs, including Fox, Sheridan and Burke, who were all friends of the Prince, and who fully expected to be asked by him to form a new government.

Mrs Fitzherbert was not an ambitious woman, and politics were a wholly alien sphere to her. But now, for the first and last time in her

🜲 *Rowlandson's 'Exhibition stare case', showing ladies and gentlemen cascading down the Royal Academy stairs* above, *pokes fun at George's 'artistic' social set*

British Museum/Weidenfeld Archives

🜲*The Prince of Wales's gluttony, drunkenness and general debauchery made him a ready target for cartoonists* left

🜲*In the wake of the French Revolution* right, *displays of princely extravagance became highly unpopular*

©RMN

life, she threw herself behind the Prince in his bid for power. She knew that should the Whigs assume control of the government, the Prince would at last be in a position to make amends for the public denial of their marriage, even to the point of repealing the Royal Marriage Act to enable them to live openly as man and wife.

In the event – after the House of Commons had passed a Regency Bill severely limiting the Prince's powers and the possibility of redress for Mrs Fitzherbert – the King recovered. The crisis was over, though the bitter aftertaste would linger between the Prince and the King and Queen. The Prince had also missed the best

chance he would ever have of legitimizing his marriage with Mrs Fitzherbert.

Though they would remain on good terms for several more years, the passion was fading between the Prince and his 'White Rose' as surely as the youth was draining from their looks. The Regency crisis had left George embittered and restless. Unable to play an active role in politics, as he felt his rank and age demanded, he dissipated his energies in the ways that came most naturally to him.

The debauched Prince

The Times condemned the Prince as a hard drinker and whoremonger, and his friend Sheridan described him as 'too much every lady's man to be the man of any lady'. Mrs Fitzherbert had long known this, and accepted it as if she were indulging the naughtiness of a child. She had forgiven his affairs with Lucy Howard – whose son, allegedly the Prince's, died very young and was buried at Brighton – and a singer called Anna Maria Crouch, but she put her foot down over his growing infatuation with the well-known society beauty, Lady Jersey.

Under Lady Jersey's influence, the Prince wrote to Mrs Fitzherbert saying he could never see her again, whereupon Mrs Fitzherbert left home without replying to his letter. When he discovered she had fled, he tried in vain to track her down. Though he had declared his love for another woman, the reality of life without Mrs Fitzherbert was hard to bear.

A marriage of convenience

Meanwhile, the Prince's debts were once more getting out of hand and he decided to take the step he had so often contemplated but shrunk from in the past. He would contract a marriage of convenience. His chosen bride was his first cousin, Princess Caroline of Brunswick. She was a plain, rather vulgar woman, who reputedly needed lessons in personal hygiene as well as manners before she was considered ready to meet the Prince in the spring of 1795.

It was a cynical arrangement from the first, and one in which Lady Jersey readily connived. The Prince had seen to it that Lady Jersey was appointed Princess Caroline's Lady of the Bedchamber, so that they could continue as lovers despite the marriage. When Princess Caroline was first introduced to the Prince, he turned from her without saying a word and said to one of his attendants, 'Harris, I am not well. Pray, get me a glass of brandy.' At the wedding, on 8 April 1795, the Prince was so drunk he could barely stand up. That night, he fell asleep in the fireplace, but not before giving her the child that had been one of the objects of the arranged union.

Their daughter, Princess Charlotte, was

⚜ *Mrs Fitzherbert's ample figure was a frequent butt for satire below. Here, Gillray shows Maria strapping her generous bosom into a corset to make a pair of 'patent bolsters'. On the wall is a portrait of the Prince of Wales*

PATENT-BOLSTERS:– *Le moyen d'etre en bon point!*

Mansell

born on 7 January 1796. Though he felt genuine happiness at the event, George's feelings for Princess Caroline had deteriorated so badly that he could not bear to be in her presence. He would, he said, rather see toads and vipers crawling over his food than sit at the same table as her. By the end of May, the Prince had secured a formal separation from his wife.

Beloved Maria

He was growing tired of Lady Jersey, too. In his heart of hearts, he had never stopped loving Mrs Fitzherbert, and now he made another bid to win her back. Three days after the birth of his daughter, the Prince had fallen so ill he believed himself on the point of death, and he hurriedly wrote out his will. In this long and profuse document he bequeathed everything he owned to his 'beloved and adored Maria Fitzherbert', adding, 'to her, who is called the Princess of Wales, I leave one shilling'. Four years later he admitted that the relief he felt when he had finished writing the will 'certainly did restore one in a manner to life after a dangerous and precarious illness'.

This was the beginning of a fresh campaign

♔ *Fortified by several stiff drinks, the Prince found the courage to go through with his wedding to Caroline of Brunswick, which took place in front of a candle-lit altar at the Chapel Royal in St James's Palace on 8 April 1795* above. *The marriage was to prove very short-lived: soon after the birth of their daughter, the Prince of Wales and his wife ceased living together*

♔ *Lady Jersey* left, *a handsome grandmother nine years the Prince's senior, claimed first place in his affections for two years. But although she succeeded in driving a wedge between George and Maria, the Prince's older attachment eventually reasserted itself* to bring Mrs Fitzherbert back to him but, though he showered her with declarations of love and pleas for forgiveness, she had set her heart against him and refused to see him. When he heard she was ill and her life was in danger, he fired off a letter that was extraordinarily gushing even by the Prince's standards. 'If you wish my life you shall have it,' he wrote, underscoring the words several times. 'Oh! God! Oh, God, Who

George's brothers were also embroiled in scandal. In 1811 it was alleged that the Duke of York, who was Commander-in-Chief of the Army, had allowed his mistress to act as a broker in the sale of military promotions, and that he had shared the proceeds. The cartoonists had a field day right

Mansell

'MINNEY' SEYMOUR

After Mrs Fitzherbert separated for the last time from the Prince of Wales, she devoted herself to her adopted daughter, Mary 'Minney' Seymour, the youngest child of Lord Hugh and Lady Horatia Seymour who had both died in 1801 when Minney was still a baby. While the Prince and Mrs Fitzherbert were still together they both came to look on Minney as if she were their own, though the suggestion that she was the result of the Prince's brief union with Lady Horatia seems unlikely. The Prince, whom Minney called 'Prinny', continued to see her after he had separated from Mrs Fitzherbert and they remained on extremely close terms. In fact, the Prince showed considerably more affection to Minney than he ever did to Princess Charlotte. When she was 12, Minney wrote to him: 'Dear Prinny, I am much obliged to you for your nice letter and very pretty presents...What a naughty personage you are dear Prinny to send me such new years [sic] gifts.' Minney grew into an attractive young woman, and married Colonel George Dawson in 1825

Mansell

THE GUARDIAN-ANGEL — *the hint taken from the Revᵈ Mr Peter's sublime Idea of 'an Angel conducting the Soul of a Child to Heaven'*

---

has seen the agony of my soul and knowest the purity of my intentions, have mercy on me: turn once more, I conjure thee, the heart of my Maria, to me, for whom I have lived and for whom I will die...You know you are my wife, the wife of my heart and soul.'

It would have been a hard-hearted woman who failed to respond to such entreaties, but Mrs Fitzherbert was not about to relent completely. Instead she asked for time to consider her position. The pressure on her grew intense as she tried to make up her mind, for now both of their families were urging her to agree to a reunion. The Prince's brother, Prince Edward, acted as a go-between. On 17 July 1799, after a 'very long tête-à-tête' with her, Prince Edward told his anxious brother that if he was 'any judge at all of the business', a reconciliation would 'ere long be accomplished'.

The Pope's endorsement

The sticking point for Mrs Fitzherbert was the legal status of her marriage. The embarrassment of having her virtue impugned in Parliament had wounded her deeply, but if the Roman Catholic Church would endorse the legality of the secret wedding, she would feel free to return to the Prince. To this end, she commissioned a Catholic priest, William Nassau, to go to Rome to set out the details of her case before the Pope and ask where her duty lay.

The Pope's verdict on the religious and legal complexities of the marriage was a favourable one. By March of 1800, the Prince and Mrs Fitzherbert were back together, though from now on it was to be a strictly platonic relationship. 'We live like brother and sister,' Maria told her friend Lady Anne Lindsay. 'I find no resentment though plenty of regret that I will have it on this footing and no other.'

'You know you are my wife, the wife of my heart and soul'

THE PRINCE OF WALES TO MRS FITZHERBERT

♛ *Relations between Princess Caroline and her daughter Charlotte were not as harmonious as this idealized portrait of the pair* below *suggests*

♛ *The Prince left his mark on the capital: Regent Street* right *was part of his plan for a 'Royal Mile' stretching from Portland Place to Carlton House*

Mansell

By gracious permission of HM the Queen

A HAPPY INTERLUDE

Mrs Fitzherbert described the next few years as the happiest she spent with the Prince. Brighton was still a great favourite with both of them, and they passed as much time there as they could, enjoying each other's company.

Both had grown contentedly fat, not least on account of the magnificent dinners they held each evening at the Pavilion. 'Such music, such brilliant conversation, such a profusion of luxuries,' recalled one guest. Another, rather uncharitably, described Mrs Fitzherbert at this time as 'about fifty, very fat but with a charming countenance, her features are beautiful, except her mouth which is ugly, having a set of not good false teeth...She makes a great display of a very white but not prettily formed bosom, which I often long to throw a handkerchief over.'

A new love affair

By 1808, the Prince was spending less and less time at Brighton, which he declared was 'too cold' for him, and showing a preference for Cheltenham. This change was less to do with climate, however, than with the attractions of a rich, avowedly Protestant and Tory lady called Isabella, Lady Hertford, whose country seat at Ragley in Warwickshire was a convenient distance from Cheltenham. The Prince had recently had several inconsequential affairs that Maria sensibly chose to ignore, but Lady Hertford was different. At first she repelled George's advances, but her coldness only made her more attractive to the Prince. It was soon obvious that he was in love with her.

Mrs Fitzherbert was not prepared to be publicly humiliated. She eventually delivered an ultimatum. His affair with Lady Hertford, she wrote, 'has quite destroyed the entire comfort and happiness of both our lives; it has so completely destroyed mine, that neither my health nor my spirits can bear it any longer...The purport of my writing to you is to implore you to come to a resolution...You must decide, and that decision must be done immediately.' But the Prince was unable or unwilling to decide, and so Mrs Fitzherbert declared that she was no longer prepared to see him.

In 1810, the King again fell ill, plunging the country into another Regency crisis. This time, he did not recover his reason, and on the morning of 5 February 1811 the Prince was sworn in as Regent in a ceremony at Carlton House. Five months later, in June, there occurred an episode that made it impossible for Mrs Fitzherbert ever to return to him.

The Prince was holding a grand dinner at Carlton House to celebrate his Regency. The exiled King Louis XVIII of France and his family were to be guests of honour. Mrs Fitzherbert received an invitation, but the Prince told her that there would be a new seating arrangement. For nearly 30 years, he had insisted on Mrs Fitzherbert being seated by his side at formal dinners. Now he proposed to seat people strictly according to rank, which meant that Mrs Fitzherbert would be at the end of the table. To add insult to injury, her successor in the Prince's affections, Lady Hertford, was to be seated next to the Prince instead of her. Mrs Fitzherbert refused the invitation, and from that moment on their separation was irrevocable and complete.

🗔 *The Prince was delighted to hear of Wellington's victory at Waterloo* above, *and for some time afterwards he acted as though he had been personally responsible for the military success. He hinted to the Chancellor that he should be rewarded with an increased allowance, but Parliament voted to show its gratitude to the Duke of Wellington instead*

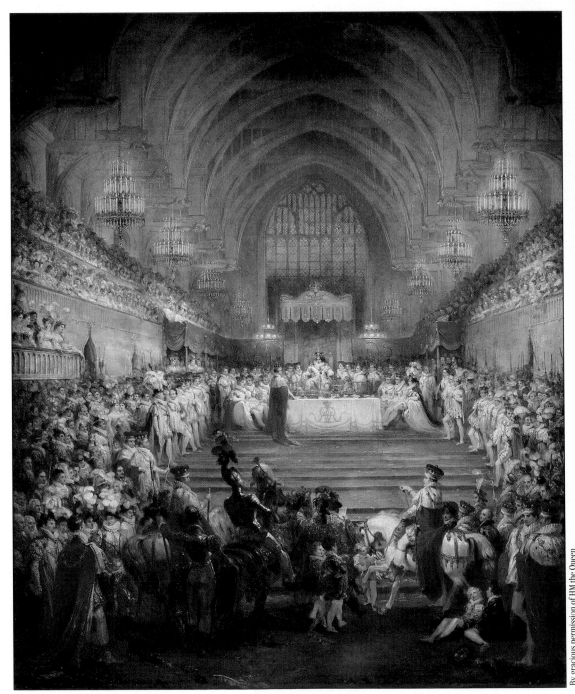

🗔 *George IV planned the most magnificent pageant for his Coronation* left. *The ceremony at Westminster Abbey lasted five hours, and the Archbishop of York preached a rousing sermon on the necessity for the sovereign to preserve his subjects' morality. Neither Mrs Fitzherbert nor Queen Caroline was invited to attend the event, although Caroline made an unsuccessful attempt to gatecrash*

By gracious permission of HM the Queen

George IV was to try to divorce his official wife, now Queen Caroline, on the grounds of adultery. But the Queen had popular opinion and sympathy in her favour, and the project was abandoned for fear of revolution. The following year, after being barred from her husband's Coronation, she died, broken and humiliated. She had asked for the inscription 'Caroline of Brunswick, the injured Queen of England' to be placed on her coffin, but the King refused this last request.

Compassionate concern

Nine years later Mrs Fitzherbert was to have her last contact with George IV, when his constitution finally succumbed to a lifetime of abuse and he fell mortally ill. She had never forgiven his treatment of her, and was not inclined to write at first, knowing as she did 'that the King always liked to make himself out worst to excite compassion'. When she discovered he was seriously ill, however, she wrote to him one last time, saying 'after so many years of continual silence, my anxiety respecting your Majesty has got the better of my scruples, and I trust your Majesty will believe me most sincere when I assure you how truly I have grieved to hear of your suffering'.

The King rallied briefly on receipt of the letter, but in the early hours of 26 June 1830, after exclaiming to his attendant, 'My dear boy! This is death!' he died. The post-mortem showed that the cause of death was arteriosclerosis, and one close friend added that a contributory cause was 'over excitement and high living'. He was

For the rest of her life Mrs Fitzherbert divided her time between London and Brighton, whose inhabitants always kept a special place in their hearts for her. 'One reason why Mrs Fitzherbert may like this place is that she is treated as queen at least of Brighton,' wrote John Croker, a friend of the Prince. 'They don't Highness her in her domestic circle but they Madam her prodigiously, and stand up longer for her arrival than for ordinary folks, and in short, go as near to acknowledging her for Princess as they can.'

Final arrangements

Mrs Fitzherbert and the Prince corresponded occasionally, but their letters were confined to practical matters, usually money. The Prince had certainly treated her dreadfully, but he was not a mean man, and he also endeavoured to keep his promises. On their marriage he had pledged to pay her an annuity of £10,000, a figure he did not always keep to, though she was never less than comfortably off. Occasionally, too, they would meet by accident in Brighton, when they would exchange frosty glances.

On 29 January 1820, the Prince Regent finally became King at the age of 57, when his father died at Windsor. One of his first acts as

THE INJURED QUEEN

The King never gave his marriage a chance to work. Having given Caroline a child, he wished earnestly to be rid of her, and to that end he contrived in 1806 to make her alleged sexual indiscretions the subject of a Commission of Enquiry. Princess Caroline had a robust sense of humour, and is reported to have said that the only adultery she had committed was with Mrs Fitzherbert's husband. The attempt to discredit her failed, but the Prince would not give up. In 1820, immediately following George IV's accession to the throne, she found her morals once more under scrutiny when a public enquiry was set up to consider her alleged affair with an Italian named Bartolomeo Pergami, who had become her constant companion

♔ *The day before his funeral, the King's body lay in state at Windsor Castle in the State Apartments, which were draped in black below. Although there was not much public display of grief at the funeral itself, the ceremony was impressive. The route of the cortège was lit by burning flambeaux held by Grenadier Guardsmen and the procession was led by trumpeters, drummers and fifers; a fitting epitaph for a King who had adored splendour. When she heard of his death, Mrs Fitzherbert shed tears in private for the man she had loved for 40 years. But the three wedding rings on her own funeral effigy right make a public allusion to her secret marriage. She died seven years after George and was buried in a Catholic church in Brighton*

buried on 15 July at Windsor. Few mourned his passing. Indeed, *The Times* opined that 'there never was an individual less regretted by his fellow-creatures than this deceased King'. This judgment was a little harsh, however. Though he made few friends and many enemies in public life, the many people close to him knew him to have been a remarkable figure in many ways – in the words of his friend the Duke of Wellington, 'the most extraordinary compound of talent, wit, buffoonery, obstinacy and good feeling – in short a medley of the most opposite qualities, with a great preponderance of good – that I ever saw in any character in my life'.

None had known him better than Mrs Fitzherbert, and he had loved no-one better than her. As the King lay in his open coffin before the funeral, the Duke of Wellington noticed a locket suspended round his neck on a black ribbon. Overcome by curiosity, he opened the locket to reveal the image of Mrs Fitzherbert. When Mrs Fitzherbert was told of this, she reportedly said not a word, but presently 'some large tears fell from her eyes'.